NATIONALISM

Malcolm Yapp

Greenhaven World History Program

GENERAL EDITORS

Malcolm Yapp
Margaret Killingray
Edmund O'Connor

Cover design by Gary Rees

ISBN 0-89908-202-5 Paper Edition
ISBN 0-89908-227-0 Library Edition

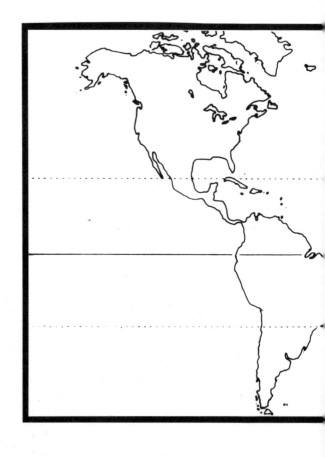

First published in Great Britain 1976 by
GEORGE G. HARRAP & CO. LTD
© George G. Harrap & Co. Ltd. 1976

NATIONALISM

by Malcolm Yapp

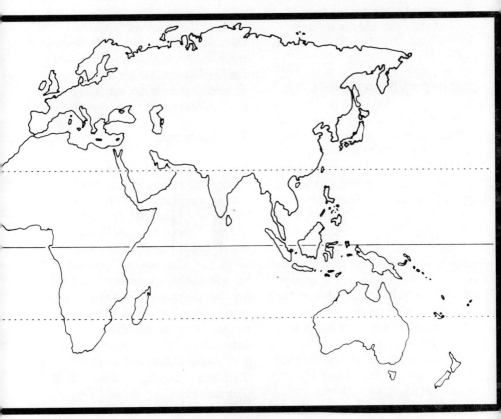

Greenhaven Press, Inc.
577 SHOREVIEW PARK ROAD
ST. PAUL, MN 55112

In 1974 138 states were members of the United Nations. Most of these states did not exist two hundred years ago. Why are there so many separate states and why have so many of these states come into being in the last two hundred years?

Part of the answer to these questions lies in the word 'nationalism'. Nationalism means the wish of a group of people to live in a state of their own. In this booklet we shall look at the sorts of groups of people who have wanted states of their own and the reasons why they have wanted them.

GROUPS AND NATIONS (D1)*

In everyday life each one of us belongs to many groups, or sets, as those who study modern mathematics call them. We cannot help belonging to some of these groups because we were born into them; for example, if you were born in London you will always belong to the group of people who were born in London even if you go to live elsewhere. Some groups, such as our schools are chosen for us. Others, such as our jobs or which football team we support, we choose for ourselves.

But what sort of group are the people who live in a state? Many would say they were British (or French or Chinese) because they happened to be born there. But if that were the only answer states would never have changed and we know that they have.

One way in which people change their states is by going to live in another state. The United States, Canada, Australia and many other countries were made in this way. *(Population).** * Another way in which people have their states changed for them is when they are beaten in a war and the victors make a new state. This is what happened in much of Africa and the Middle East. *(Traditional Africa, Ataturk)* A third way in which states change is when the people who live in them decide to break up the old state and make new ones out of it. This last way is usually called nationalism.

Not all groups want states of their own. There has never been a state for people with red hair, or for bricklayers, or for everyone named Smith. What sort of groups do want states of their own?

1 Language

At the end of the eighteenth century Germany was divided among many states. Some men put forward the idea that all Germans should live in one state which should be for Germans only. But what was a German? He was not just someone who lived in Germany: he was someone who spoke German as his mother tongue. The early German nationalists believed that the group which should form the state was a language group (D2). *(Bismarck)*

This idea, that the language group was the most important factor in making a state, became one of the main features of national movements, and in one way or another affected almost all states during the nineteenth and twentieth centuries. It is present

*The reference (D) indicates the numbered documents at the end of this book.
* *Titles in brackets refer to other booklets in the Program

The United Nations Building in New York

3

in Arab nationalism (D3), Turkish nationalism, and most European nationalisms including those of the Irish and Welsh (D4).

2 Geography

Another early national movement was that of Italy. Though the Italians spoke one language Giuseppe Mazzini (1805-72), one of the leading Italian nationalists, thought that 'geography' made Italy. He believed that God had made mountains and rivers to divide people into separate nations and that these nations should become states (D5).

Geography was to be another reason why people came to decide

Welsh nationalists demand that all road signs in their country should be in Welsh

Giuseppe Mazzini, the Italian nationalist writer

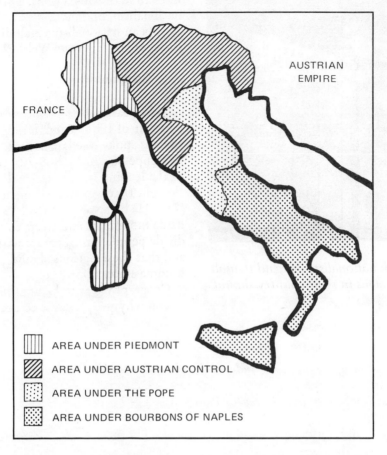

FRANCE

AUSTRIAN
EMPIRE

|||| AREA UNDER PIEDMONT

//// AREA UNDER AUSTRIAN CONTROL

::: AREA UNDER THE POPE

::: AREA UNDER BOURBONS OF NAPLES

that they should have their own
states especially in those countries
which, like Italy, had a natural
geographical unity: some because
they were made by a large river
like Egypt; some because they
were cut off from their neighbours
by mountains, like Switzerland;
and some, like Britain, because
they were islands (D6).

3   History

A third factor which made people
think of themselves as separate

nations was their history. At the
end of the eighteenth century
Poland was divided among the
neighbouring states of Prussia,
Austria and Russia. But the Poles
did not forget that they had once
had their own state and continued
to struggle to get it back until
finally they succeeded in 1918.
Italians were encouraged by their
thoughts of the Roman Empire.
Greeks took heart from the history
of ancient Greece during their
struggle against Ottoman rule from
1821 to 1829 (D7).

The Battle of Navarino, 1827. The defeat of the Ottoman fleet by European ships led to the independence of Greece

Muslim refugees leave India for Pakistan in 1947

4 Religion

Religion was another reason for people demanding a state of their own. *(Religion)* In south-eastern Europe during the nineteenth century most people were Christians but they lived under the rule of the Ottomans who were Muslims. *(Suleyman and the Ottoman Empire)* The fact that they were Christians helped the Greeks, Bulgarians, Romanians and Serbs to see themselves as different from their Muslim Ottoman rulers. In Asia many of the national movements began as religious movements: Burmese nationalism began as a Buddhist reaction to Christian British rule; Indonesian nationalism as a Muslim reaction to Christian Dutch rule. But perhaps the best example comes from the history of Pakistan.

When India was ruled by Britain about two thirds of its people were Hindus and one third Muslims. When the Indian national movement began in the late nineteenth century the early leaders said little about religion and talked about the unity of all Indians (D8). *(Indian Nationalism)* But most of them were Hindus and in their effort to get more support from ordinary people some leaders began to appeal to the people as Hindus. This worried the Muslims who formed the Muslim League to look after the interests of Muslims. Despite many attempts to bring Hindus and Muslims together in an Indian nation the religious differences were too strong, so when India became independent of British rule in 1947 it was divided into two states: one was called

India in which most of the people were Hindus; and the other Pakistan in which most people were Muslims (D9, 10). *(Gandhi)*

The story did not end in 1947, however, and what happened afterwards helps us to understand more about nationalism. Most of the Muslims in British India had lived in two areas; the north west and the north east. In 1947 these two areas became West and East Pakistan; one state but two countries a thousand miles apart. Pakistan existed only because of religion: it had no history as a state, no geographical unity, and the people spoke different languages — mainly Punjabi and Sindhi in the West and Bengali in the East. Despite every effort to get people to think of themselves as Pakistanis and to speak one language (Urdu) the differences between East and West increased, until the East rebelled and broke away to form the independent state of Bangladesh in 1972. Religion had been enough to make Pakistan but on its own religion was not enough to hold the state together; language differences, in particular, pulled Pakistan apart.

5 Race

Another way in which people have felt that they belonged to one nation has been when they have thought of themselves as one race. 'Race' is not a very useful word because it is used to mean many different things. But there are some groups who are obviously different from others, for example, people of different colours. In the United States about twenty million people

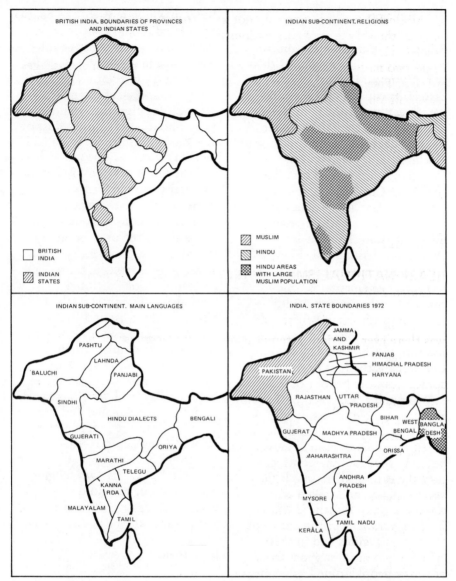

THE EFFECT OF LANGUAGE AND RELIGION ON THE INDIAN SUB-CONTINENT

(10 per cent of the population) are the descendants of Negro slaves. They were treated differently from and worse than white people, and many came to feel that they were not ordinary Americans but black Americans. Some began to support the idea of black nationalism (D11). In Africa also differences of colour have been important in making people think of themselves as national groups and want to form independent states free from white control.

A Black Power demonstration in New York, 1970

(Nyerere and Nkrumah) In the West Indies racial differences between Indians and Negroes also produced rival nationalisms (D12, 13).

The story of modern Israel provides an example of a different sort of nationalism not connected with colour. Two thousand years ago most Jews lived in Palestine. Later they became scattered in many places, mainly in the Middle East and eastern Europe. At the end of the nineteenth century many east European Jews began to leave that area for western Europe and, especially, the United States. A few began a movement to return to Palestine in order to build a new Jewish state there (D14). This movement was called Zionism. When Palestine came under British rule after the First World War many east European Jews went

there. By 1947 there were nearly 500,000 Jews in Palestine and the independent state of Israel was formed. After that Jews came to Palestine from many areas, especially from other parts of the Middle East.

Although the Jews had a religion — Judaism — Zionism was not just a religious movement. Many Jews were not Zionists and were content to practise their religion in the countries in which they lived (D15). On the other hand, religion was not important to some Zionists. Many Jews thought of themselves as a race and, what is perhaps more important, other people regarded them in the same way. It was because they were seen as a different race, not just a different religion, that they were treated so badly in certain countries in

The Wailing Wall in Jerusalem has great emotional importance for Jews

Europe, especially in Nazi Germany (D16). *(Hitler's Reich)* This bad treatment strengthened their wish to have a state of their own.

Israeli Jews had a religion, a history, and other things in common. They also had a sense of unity against the Arabs who did not want a Jewish state in Palestine. But at first they had neither one language nor one way of life. To strengthen their national feeling they decided to develop a language of their own (Modern Hebrew) and, by work, education and army service, to try to build a single way of life for all Israelis.

6   Anti-Colonialism

We have seen that language, geography, history, religion and race can all help to make groups of people think of themselves as nations and want to have a state of their own. But there are many new states whose people do not have any of these things in common. Several of these states are in parts of Asia, Africa and South America. The people of these areas have something else in common: they all lived for a time under European rule. *(Imperialism)* Dislike of being ruled from outside can make people co-operate to form an independent state.

7   Nation Building

Even though people may come together to form a state this does not necessarily make them into a nation, so when such states are formed the governments of them try to create in their people a feeling that they all belong to the same group and want to be members of the same state. These governments do this in the same way as the Israeli Government: getting people to live and work together, learn in the same schools, serve in the same army, thus developing a sense of shared history and a shared future. This process of turning people into a nation is sometimes called nation building (D19). We could say that nationalism is the wish of a group of people to have a state of their own, and nation building represents the wish of a group of people who form a state to have a nation of their own. The idea is to make the state and the nation the same.

Often states which are trying to turn themselves into nations run into trouble. After they became independent two of the largest states in Africa, the Congo (Zaire) and Nigeria, almost broke up into smaller states because many of the people who had joined together to win their independence from Belgium and Britain did not think they had enough in common to go on living together in the same state. In both states there was much fighting before those who wanted one state in each country won.

WHY NATIONALISM?

We have looked at some of the things which people who make nation states have in common. But you will say that most of these people had all these things for a very long time before they began to say that their language, religion or race were reasons why they should have states of their own.

A Nigerian Federal soldier during the 1967 civil war. Nation building in Africa requires strong armies

The Germans have always spoken German but it was only at the end of the eighteenth century that they began to say that this was a reason why they should all live in the same state. The Italians have always lived in Italy but not until the nineteenth century did this seem a good reason for them to have one state there. Why did nationalism appear only at the end of the eighteenth century?

Many historians have tried to answer that question and they do not agree on the answer. Here we will look at some of the main answers they have given.

1   Nationalism is natural

When people began to discuss nationalism in the nineteenth century, many, like Mazzini, thought that it was obviously a good thing, even that nations had been designed by God. So they did not think it necessary to explain what nationalism was; only why nation states had not always existed. Their answer to that was simple: bad men and bad governments had prevented them from existing. All that was necessary was to get rid of the bad men and the bad governments and nation states would come into being automatically and everyone would live happily ever after.

If that had happened we might have accepted their explanation that nationalism was natural. But if we look at the history of the last two hundred years we find that millions of people have been killed in the name of nationalism. Wars have been fought because different people had different ideas

Giuseppe Garibaldi, the Italian nationalist soldier who freed southern Italy

about where the frontiers of nation states should run. Breaking up old states was a very bloody business: many people died when India was divided between India and Pakistan and when the Ottoman Empire was broken up (D20). New nation states were often very brutal in their behaviour to those who did not belong to the group which formed the nation (D21). There are very few states in which everyone is the same colour, speaks the same language, has the same religion. In most states there are groups of people called minorities, who think of themselves or are regarded as different from the

POBLACHT NA H EIREANN.

THE PROVISIONAL GOVERNMENT
OF THE
IRISH REPUBLIC
TO THE PEOPLE OF IRELAND.

IRISHMEN AND IRISHWOMEN : In the name of God and of the dead generations from which she receives her old tradition of nationhood, Ireland, through us, summons her children to her flag and strikes for her freedom.

Having organised and trained her manhood through her secret revolutionary organisation, the Irish Republican Brotherhood, and through her open military organisations, the Irish Volunteers and the Irish Citizen Army, having patiently perfected her discipline, having resolutely waited for the right moment to reveal itself, she now seizes that moment, and, supported by her exiled children in America and by gallant allies in Europe, but relying in the first on her own strength, she strikes in full confidence of victory.

We declare the right of the people of Ireland to the ownership of Ireland, and to the unfettered control of Irish destinies, to be sovereign and indefeasible. The long usurpation of that right by a foreign people and government has not extinguished the right, nor can it ever be extinguished except by the destruction of the Irish people. In every generation the Irish people have asserted their right to national freedom and sovereignty ; six times during the past three hundred years they have asserted it in arms. Standing on that fundamental right and again asserting it in arms in the face of the world, we hereby proclaim the Irish Republic as a Sovereign Independent State, and we pledge our lives and the lives of our comrades-in-arms to the cause of its freedom, of its welfare, and of its exaltation among the nations.

The Irish Republic is entitled to, and hereby claims, the allegiance of every Irishman and Irishwoman. The Republic guarantees religious and civil liberty, equal rights and equal opportunities to all its citizens, and declares its resolve to pursue the happiness and prosperity of the whole nation and of all its parts, cherishing all the children of the nation equally, and oblivious of the differences carefully fostered by an alien government, which have divided a minority from the majority in the past.

Until our arms have brought the opportune moment for the establishment of a permanent National Government, representative of the whole people of Ireland and elected by the suffrages of all her men and women, the Provisional Government, hereby constituted, will administer the civil and military affairs of the Republic in trust for the people.

We place the cause of the Irish Republic under the protection of the Most High God, Whose blessing we invoke upon our arms, and we pray that no one who serves that cause will dishonour it by cowardice, inhumanity, or rapine. In this supreme hour the Irish nation must, by its valour and discipline and by the readiness of its children to sacrifice themselves for the common good, prove itself worthy of the august destiny to which it is called.

Signed on Behalf of the Provisional Government,

THOMAS J. CLARKE.

SEAN Mac DIARMADA. THOMAS MacDONAGH.

P. H. PEARSE. EAMONN CEANNT.

JAMES CONNOLLY. JOSEPH PLUNKETT.

The Proclamation of the Irish Republic, 24th April 1916, which led to an armed struggle for independence from Britain

The Battle of Magenta, 1859. The defeat of Austria by France helped to achieve the eventual unification of northern Italy

majority. A few states try to make it possible for minorities to live their own lives, although not all minorities are content with this. Other states try to get rid of their minorities by forcing them to be like the majority, or by throwing them out, or even by murdering them as the Nazis did with the Jews in Europe.

Because of this nationalism has a bad name and the old idea that it was necessarily good is often doubted.

2   Nationalism is unnatural

The second theory follows from this experience of nationalism.

Nationalism, say some historians, is unnatural: it was invented by evil men to suit their own personal ends and copied by others for the same reason, or because men are like sheep and follow fashions in ideas as they follow fashions in clothes. So once again it is not necessary to explain nationalism; it is enough to say that some men are bad and others easily led astray.

The difficulty with this theory is that it does not explain why nationalism appeared only at the end of the eighteenth century or why evil men should have chosen nationalism as a way of getting what they wanted.

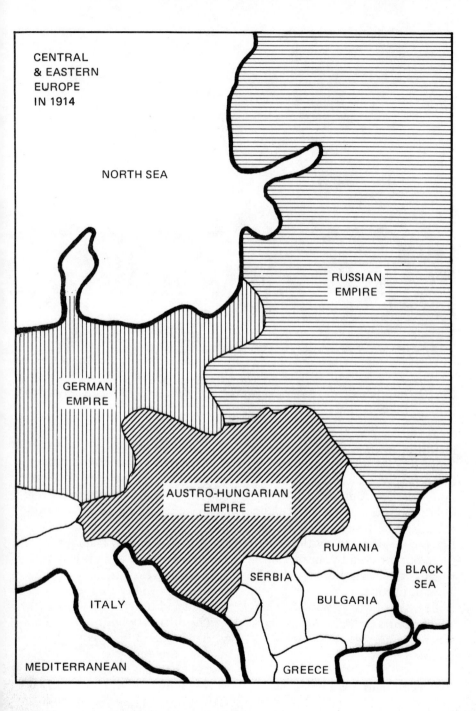

CENTRAL
& EASTERN
EUROPE
IN 1914

NORTH SEA

RUSSIAN
EMPIRE

GERMAN
EMPIRE

AUSTRO-HUNGARIAN
EMPIRE

RUMANIA

SERBIA

BLACK
SEA

BULGARIA

ITALY

MEDITERRANEAN

GREECE

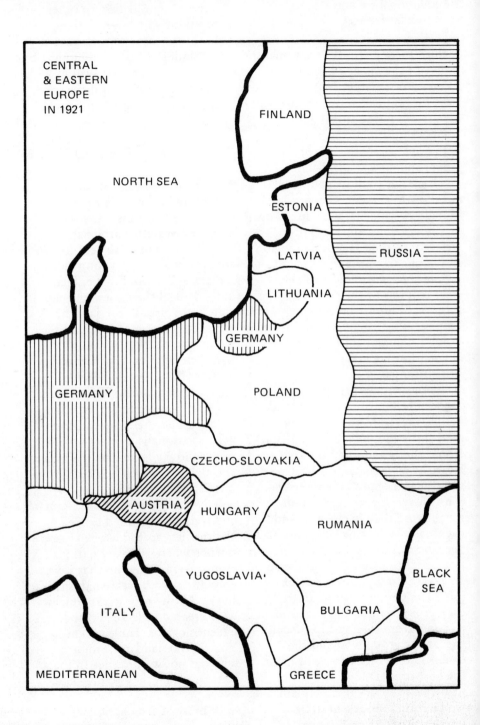

CENTRAL
& EASTERN
EUROPE
IN 1921

FINLAND

NORTH SEA

ESTONIA

LATVIA

RUSSIA

LITHUANIA

GERMANY

GERMANY

POLAND

CZECHO-SLOVAKIA

AUSTRIA

HUNGARY

RUMANIA

YUGOSLAVIA·

BLACK
SEA

ITALY

BULGARIA

MEDITERRANEAN

GREECE

3　Nationalism and modernization

A third theory says that nationalism is part of the change from traditional to modern societies. In other booklets you can read about traditional societies and traditional governments. Traditional governments left people alone to run their own affairs and, as a result, it did not much matter to most people who ran the government. Often traditional governments were made up of a minority who were quite different in their language, religion and habits from the majority of the people they ruled. Most of the great empires of the past were like this, for example the Roman Empire, (Pax Romana) the Ottoman Empire, the Mongol Empire, the Mughal Empire and even the British Empire.

When societies began to modernize the situation changed. People moved to towns, learned to read and write, mixed with people from other groups and became aware of differences, especially when they began to compete for jobs. Governments began to do much more than in the past and eventually it became very important who ran the government, because if it were not your group you could find yourself out of a job. (The Growth of the State) So each group wanted the government to come from their group. Usually the largest group won and the others had to break away or make the best of it (D22).

This last theory does explain why nationalism began to be important at the end of the eighteenth century because it links the rise of nationalism to other revolutions which were taking place at the same time in government, industry and communications. It was these other revolutions which made people aware of differences which had previously not seemed important.

THE SPREAD OF NATIONALISM

Nationalism spread throughout the world in the wake of the other modern revolutions. Like them it began in western Europe at the end of the eighteenth century. In some west European countries including Britain, France, Spain and Portugal the nation and the state were already roughly the same, so these states avoided the worst disturbances, although they had their problems with minority groups (Britain with Ireland, Scotland and Wales; France with the Bretons; and Spain with the Catalans and the Basques). Elsewhere nationalism broke up old states and made new ones. Holland and Belgium which had been joined in 1815 split in 1830; Norway and Sweden split in 1905. Germany and Italy were unified by 1870. Nationalism spread later in eastern Europe where so many national groups were mixed up that it was very difficult to create national states. All the new states which were created in 1918 (Poland, Czechoslovakia, Hungary and Yugoslavia) had large minorities who did not want to live in the state in which they found themselves.

In most of Asia nationalism became important in the twentieth century. In China (The Chinese

Revolution; Mao Tse-tung) and Japan *(Japan's Modernization)* most of the people felt that they belonged to these two states, but elsewhere the building of new states was a difficult process, especially in South Asia and in the Middle East. In most of Africa nationalism grew quickly only after 1950.

War has been very important in the history of nationalist movements. Modern states can often put down nationalist movements by force. On the other hand, nation-alists succeed more often when the power of the old state has been weakened through defeat in war. The First World War was particularly significant in this way because the defeat of Austria, Germany and the Ottoman Empire meant that their lands could be divided up to make new states. *(The Two World Wars)* The Second World War was also important because it loosened the hold of Britain, France and Holland over parts of Asia, and made it easier for nationalists to replace them.

Part of the border between East and West Germany. United in 1870, Germany was again divided in 1945

The threat of war could also make it more difficult for nationalists to get what they wanted. If a state breaks up, the balance between the others may be upset and war between them may become more likely. Because of this danger many states do not like helping nationalists. This factor helped Nigeria and the Congo to survive and made it very difficult for the Kurds of Iraq, Iran and Turkey to gain their independence. Sometimes it suits great powers to keep other nations divided; the Cold War has kept Germany and Korea each divided into two states. (The Cold War)

When we speak of nationalists we are usually thinking of educated nationalist leaders who lived in towns. Many of their people were peasants who understood little of what their leaders said. A story is told about a professor who was sent to settle frontiers in eastern Europe after the First World War. When he asked villagers what was their nationality they could not understand. When he asked if they were Hungarians, Poles, Czechs, Slovaks, or Ukrainians they simply replied 'We are from home.' But few as they were the nationalist leaders were able to decide what home meant for most of the people in the world.

NATIONALISM IN WORLD HISTORY

Nationalism has been one of the most powerful forces in modern world history because it has changed the political map of the world and the lives of millions of people. Of all the great multi-national empires of the past only those of Russia (Stalin) and possibly China survive. But nationalism has created as many problems as it has solved; there are very few states in which everyone is happy to be a citizen and many large states are still in danger of being broken up into smaller states. How many more groups of people will want states of their own and how small can states become? Or can people find a different principle to help them decide to which states they should belong?

DOCUMENT 1

STATE AND NATION   *THOMAS MASARYK – First President of Czechoslovakia, 9th October 1915*

Today we are forced to acknowledge the existence of nations and we are obliged to make a distinction between states and nations. An Englishman speaking of his nation identifies the nation and the state. Not so the Serb and the Bohemian because to his experience state and nation do not coincide, his nation being spread over several states, or sharing a state with other nations.

In the *Statesman's Yearbook* for 1915 we find in Europe twenty-eight states. If we take one of the few better ethnological maps of Europe we find sixty-two nations or nationalities. In other words in Europe we have more than twice as many nations as states, and that means that the existing states are nationally mixed, and that states must be composed of more than one nation. And that means further that there are in Europe far more dependent than independent nations.

DOCUMENT 2

LANGUAGE AND NATIONALISM   *JOHANN FICHTE (1762–1814)*
– *A German philosopher*

The first, original and truly natural frontiers of all states are undoubtedly their inner frontiers. Those who speak the same language are linked together by mere nature with a host of invisible ties, they understand each other and are capable of communicating more and more closely with one another, they belong together, they are by nature one indivisible whole. From this internal boundary the making of the external boundary according to where people live is a result. It is not because men live between certain mountains and rivers that they are a people but because they were a people already by a law of nature which is much higher.

DOCUMENT 3

ARAB NATIONALISM   *Extract from the Constitution of the Arab Renaissance Ba'ath party, one of the leading Arab nationalist political parties*

One Arab nation with a immortal Mission
The Arab Renaissance [Ba'ath] Socialist Party
A popular national revolutionary movement
Striving for Arab Unity, Freedom and Socialism.

First Principle: Unity and Freedom of the Arab Nation.

The Arabs are one nation having a natural right to live in one state and to be free to direct its affairs.

The Ba'ath party therefore considers:
1. the Arab homeland an indivisible political and economic unity and that no Arab country can live in isolation from another Arab country;
2. the Arab nation a cultural unity, and that all existing differences are incidental and false and will totally disappear with the awakening of Arab consciousness;

3. that the Arab homeland belongs to the Arabs who alone have the right to direct its affairs and utilize its resources and potentialities.

DOCUMENT 4

WELSH NATIONALISM   *W.C. ELVET THOMAS – President of the Royal National Eisteddfod, August 1972*

On every side we have seen merciless enemies threatening our heritage – and many of the enemies, alas, from among ourselves as though doing their utmost to destroy the old language and in that way to exterminate us. We are a sick nation and we cannot rid ourselves of our sickness except through self sacrifice and suffering. Thank God after centuries of loathsome civility there is rising at last a generation that puts Wales and the Welsh language first and is ready to suffer and is suffering for their sake . . . The most terrible of enemies is English television. Television is the most powerful means of communication ever devised and in Wales it pours its deadly English flood every day and night into our homes.

DOCUMENT 5

NATIONALISM AND GEOGRAPHY   *GIUSEPPE MAZZINI, 1858*

God divided Humanity into distinct groups upon the face of our globe, and thus planted the seeds of nations. Bad governments have disfigured the design of God, which you may see clearly marked out, as far, at least, as regards Europe, by the courses of the great rivers, by the lines of the lofty mountains, and by other geographical conditions; they have disfigured it by conquest, by greed, by jealousy of the just sovereignty of others; disfigured it so much that today there is perhaps no nation except England and France whose confines correspond to this design. They did not, and they do not, recognise any country except their own families and dynasties, the egoism of caste. But the divine design will infallibly be fulfilled. Natural divisions, the innate spontaneous tendencies of the peoples will replace the arbitrary divisions sanctioned by bad governments. The map of Europe will be remade.

To you who have been born in Italy, God has allotted, as if favouring you specially, the best-defined country in Europe. God has stretched round you sublime and indisputable boundaries; on one side the highest mountains of Europe, the Alps; on the other the sea.

DOCUMENT 6

ENGLISH NATIONALISM   *WILLIAM SHAKESPEARE – John of*
Gaunt in Richard II

This royal throne of kings, this scepter'd isle
This earth of majesty, this seat of Mars,
This other Eden, demi-paradise;
This fortress built by nature for herself
Against infection and the hand of war;
This happy breed of men, this little world;
This precious stone set in a silver sea,
Which serves it in the office of a wall,
Or as a moat defensive to a house,
Against the envy of less happier lands;
This blessed plot, this earth, this realm, this England.

DOCUMENT 7

HISTORY AND NATIONALISM   *Declaration of Greek Independence,*
27th January 1822

The Greek nation calls Heaven and Earth to witness that in spite of the
frightful yoke of the Ottomans, which threatened it with destruction, it
still exists. It declares today, before God and man, by the organ of its
legitimate representatives, meeting in its national congress convoked by
the people, its political independence.

Descendants of a nation distinguished by its enlightenment and by its
humane civilization, living in an age when this same civilization spreads
its benefits in life-giving profusion over the other peoples of Europe,
could the Greeks remain longer in this state?

Such were the causes of the war which we have been forced to under-
take against the Turks. Far from being founded on demagogic or rebellious
principles, far from being motivated by the selfish interests of a few
individuals, this war is a national and holy one; it aims only at the
restoration of the nation and its re-establishment in the rights of property,
honour and life. We demand only our re-establishment in the European
association, where our religion, our customs, and our position call on us
to re-unite ourselves to the great Christian family and to take once more
among the nations the rank which a usurping power has unjustly snatched
from us.

DOCUMENT 8

INDIAN NATIONALISM *G.K. GOKHALE — One of the early Indian nationalist leaders, 1905*

The growth during the last fifty years of a feeling of common nationality, based upon common tradition, common disabilities and common hopes and aspirations, has been most striking. The fact that we are Indians first and Hindus, Mohammedans, Parsees or Christians afterwards, is being realized in a steadily increasing measure, and the idea of a united and renovated India, marching onwards to a place among the nations of the world, worthy of her great past, is no longer a mere idle dream of a few imaginative minds, but is the definitely accepted creed of those who form the brain of the community — the educated classes of the country.

DOCUMENT 9

RELIGION AND NATIONALISM 1 *MUHAMMAD IQBAL — An Indian Muslim writer calls for a Muslim state, 1930*

Communalism [i.e. religious groups] is indispensible to the formation of a harmonious whole in a country like India. The units of Indian society are not territorial as in European countries. India is a continent of human groups belonging to different races, speaking different languages and professing different religions. Their behaviour is not at all determined by a common race consciousness. Even the Hindus do not form a homogeneous group. The principle of European democracy cannot be applied to India without recognizing the fact of communal groups. The Muslim demand for the creation of a Muslim India within India is therefore perfectly justified. Personally I would go further. I would like to see the Punjab, Sind and Baluchistan amalgamated into a single state. Self government within the British Empire, the formation of a consolidated Indian Muslim State, appears to me to be the final destiny of the Muslims, at least of North-West India.

DOCUMENT 10

RELIGION AND NATIONALISM II *Muhammad Iqbal's idea of an Indian Muslim state became the policy of the Muslim League, led by Muhammad Ali Jinnah. In this extract the idea is attacked by JAWAHARLAL NEHRU, the future Prime Minister of India, who believed in one Indian nation*

Mr Jinnah's demand [for a Muslim state] was based on a new theory he had recently propounded — that India consisted of two nations Hindu and Moslem. Why only two I do not know for if nationality was based on religion, then there are many nations in India. Of two brothers one may be a Hindu, another a Moslem: they would belong to two different nations. These two nations existed in varying proportions in most of the villages of India. They were nations which had no boundaries: they overlapped. A Bengali Moslem and a Bengali Hindu, living together, speaking the same language and having much the same traditions and customs belonged to different nations. All this was very difficult to grasp; it seemed a reversion to some medieval theory.

DOCUMENT 11

BLACK NATIONALISM   *MARCUS GARVEY — American Negro leader, 1921*

At no time in the history of the world, for the last five hundred years was there ever a serious attempt made to free Negroes. We have been camouflaged into believing that we were made free by Abraham Lincoln, but up to now we are still slaves, we are industrial slaves, we are social slaves, we are political slaves, and the new Negro desires a freedom that has no boundary, no limit. We desire a freedom that will lift us to the common standard of all men, whether they be white men of Europe or yellow men of Asia, therefore, in our desire to uplift ourselves to that standard we shall stop at nothing until there is a free and redeemed Africa . . . . Let the world know that 400,000,000 Negroes are prepared to die or live as free men. Despise us as much as you care. Ignore us as much as you care. We are coming 400,000,000 strong. We are coming with our woes behind us, with the memory of suffering behind us — woes and suffering of three hundred years — they shall be our inspiration.

DOCUMENT 12

RACIAL NATIONALISM IN THE WEST INDIES   The Robertson Commission *on British Guiana, 1954*

Education is now eagerly sought by Indian parents for their children; many Indians have important shares in the economic and commercial life of the colony; the rice trade is largely in their hands from production to marketing. Their very success in these spheres has begun to awaken the fears of the African section of the population, and it cannot be denied that since India received her independence in 1947 there has been a marked self-assertiveness amongst Indians in British Guiana. Guianese of African extraction were not afraid to tell us that many Indians in British Guiana looked forward to the day when British Guiana would not be part of the British Commonwealth but an East Indian Empire. The result has been a tendency for racial tension to increase. We do not altogether share the confidence of the Waddington Commision that a comprehensive loyalty to British Guiana can be stimulated among peoples of such diverse origins.

DOCUMENT 13

RACIAL TENSIONS IN THE WEST INDIES   DR CHEDDI JAGAN –
Former Chief Minister of British Guiana, describes the 1953 election campaign

We were caught also in the cross fire of race. The National Democratic Party and the League of Coloured People attempted to woo away Negro support from the People's Progressive Party [the PPP, Jagan's party] by appealing to Negro racialism. Their propaganda line was simple enough – the PPP was Indian dominated. On the other hand in the countryside the Indian voters were told that I was sacrificing the interests of the Indians and selling out to the Negroes. Crude religious and racist appeals were made by the Hindu pundits and Daniel Debidin's United Farmers' and Workers' Party respectively. The West Indies Federation provided the opportunity for these reactionaries. The line taken by Debidin's party was that Indian interests in Guiana would be lost and submerged in a Negro-dominated West Indies Federation. And so it originated the slogan 'Apan Jaat' [literally, own race]. The intention was to frighten the Indians away from supporting the PPP on the basis of racial emotionalism. It was also one of the main factors which led the PPP to call for a referendum on the question whether or not British Guiana should enter the West Indies Federation.

DOCUMENT 14

ZIONISM   THEODORE HERZL – The founder of modern Zionism, 1896

I think the Jewish question is no more a social than a religious one; it is a national question; we are a people – one people. We have honestly tried everywhere to merge ourselves in the societies in which we live and to preserve our religion. We are not permitted to do this. In countries where we have lived for centuries we are still looked down on as strangers. The majority many decide who are the strangers; might precedes right. It is useless therefore for us to be loyal patriots. If only we could be left in peace. But I think we shall not be left in peace. Everything tends in fact to the same conclusion which is clearly put in that classic Berlin phrase 'Juden raus' [Out with the Jews!] I shall now put the question in the briefest possible form: are we to get out now and where to? The whole plan is in essence perfectly simple. Let us be given sovereignty over part of the world big enough to satisfy the rightful needs of a nation; the rest we shall manage for ourselves.

DOCUMENT 15

ANTI-ZIONISM   *DR HERMAN ADLER — Chief Rabbi of England, 1878*

When we dwelt in the Holy Land we had a political organization of our own; we had judges and kings to rule over us. But ever since the conquest of Palestine by the Romans, we have ceased to be a body politic: we are citizens of the country in which we dwell. We are simply Englishmen or Frenchmen, or Germans, as the case may be . . . we stand in the same relation to our countrymen as any other religious sect, having the same stake in the national welfare and the same claim on the privileges and duties of citizens. To the question, what is the political bearing of Judaism? I would reply that Judaism has no political bearing whatever . . . religion is the main bond.

DOCUMENT 16

NATIONALISM AND RACE   *ADOLF HITLER — My Struggle*

One day I suddenly encountered a phenomenon in a long kaftan and wearing black sidelocks. My first thought was: is this a Jew? I watched the man stealthily and cautiously, but the longer I gazed at this strange face and examined it section by section, the more I asked myself: is this a German? . . . .

My inner hatred of the Habsburg [Austrian] State increased daily. This motley of Czechs, Poles, Hungarians, Ruthenians, Serbs and Croats, and always that bacillus which is the solvent of human society, the Jew, here and there and everywhere — the whole spectacle was repugnant to me.

The longer I lived in that city [Vienna] the stronger became my hatred for the promiscuous swarm of foreign peoples which had begun to batten on that old nursery ground of German culture.

DOCUMENT 17

NATIONALISM AND ANTI-COLONIALISM *SUKARNO – Former President of Indonesia in 1956*

We of Asia are told that the troubles of our continent are due to nationalism. It is true that there is unrest in Asia but that unrest is the result of colonialism and not due to the liberating effects of nationalism. I say the 'liberating effects of nationalism'. I do not mean only that nations are again free of colonial bonds but I mean that men feel themselves free. You who have never known colonialism can never appreciate what it does to man.

This I know: we of Indonesia and the citizens of many countries of Asia and Africa have seen our dearest and best suffer and die, struggle and fail, and rise again to struggle and fail again – and again be resurrected from the very earth and finally achieve their goal. Something burned in them; something inspired them. They called it nationalism. For us there is nothing ignoble in that word. On the contrary it contains for us all that is best in mankind and all that is noblest.

DOCUMENT 18

AFRICAN NATIONALISM *TOM MBOYA – A Kenya nationalist leader*

Some foreign visitors have expressed surprise about the political rallies they have seen in Africa. There is the huge crowd, streaming toward a stadium or an open piece of ground, sitting patiently for hours while a dozen politicians make speeches. The speakers do not seem to make many new points. The speeches are frequently interrupted by the speaker calling on the crowd to thunder back at him a series of slogans. The crowd is good natured, it is true, and seems to look on it as a festival occasion. But what is the point of it all?

It is easy to show the importance of these rallies. They are intended to show the colonial power the strength and unity of the people. And among the people they are intended to show the strength of the leader and the complete loyalty of his followers, and to persuade the few who doubt the rightness of the cause that after all everybody else believes in it. The rallies tackle the task, in the early days of a national 'movement, of creating among Africans a sense of self-confidence, a feeling that it is not only right to fight for his independence but that it is possible to win his independence. Further that it is not only right that he should be free, but that he has a duty to free himself.

DOCUMENT 19

NATION BUILDING IN AFRICA   *PRESIDENT NYERERE of Tanzania in 1966*

There are now thirty-six different nationalities in free Africa, one for each of the thirty-six independent states — to say nothing of the areas still under colonial or alien domination . . . . None of the nation states of Africa are 'natural' units. Our present boundaries . . . are the result of European decisions at the time of the Scramble for Africa. They are senseless; they cut across ethnic groups, often disregard natural physical divisions, and result in many different language groups being encompassed within a state. If the present states are not to disintegrate it is essential that deliberate steps be taken to foster a feeling of nationhood. Otherwise our present multitude of small countries . . . could break up into even smaller units — perhaps based on tribalism. . . . In order to fulfil its responsibilities to the people it has led to freedom, each nationalist government must develop its own economy, its own organizations and institutions, and its own dominant nationalism. . . . And the truth is that as each of us develops his own state we raise more and more barriers between ourselves. . . . Most of all we develop a national pride which could easily be inimical to the development of a pride in Africa. This is the dilemma of the Pan—Africanist in Africa now. . . .

DOCUMENT 20

NATIONALISM AND PARTITION IN INDIA   *A British offical in Bahawalpur, now part of Pakistan*

We suddenly saw a group of about a dozen villagers bobbing up and down on a sand hill some thirty yards away. One of them in the middle was holding up a stick with a little green flag tied to the end. He seemed very pleased with the flag and was gazing up at it and shouting. The others were jiggering about round him. The whole thing gave the impression of being a very feeble and absurd pro-Pakistan or pro-Muslim demonstration staged for our benefit. In somewhat harsh terms we asked the villagers what the hell they thought they were doing. The man holding the flag grinned ingratiatingly and, pointing to the miserable bit of green cloth at the end of his stick, said, 'This is our flag. We now have Pakistan and Muslim Raj'. By this time the Commissioner of Police had joined us.

'These are Hindus, ' he suddenly exclaimed. 'Look at this fellow; he's nothing but a Hindu shopkeeper. His ears are pierced. He's been wearing earrings.'

I was completely taken back, and it was only after a few seconds that it dawned upon me that these were men who within the last day or two had accepted Islam, as it were, at the point of the sword. The Hindus told us that their village had been attacked and looted the previous day by large mobs of Muslim peasants from the surrounding countryside. They had been compelled to embrace Islam in order to save their lives.

DOCUMENT 21

CONFLICTS OF NATIONALISMS   *Riots in Kuala Lumpur,*
Malaysia, May 1969

A Chinese shopkeeper was shut indoors on Thursday night when his shop was surrounded by Malays carrying torches. They demanded that he hand over the contents of his shop to them. When he refused to do this they set fire to the shop; he escaped with one child and his wife (who was injured with a parang cut as they ran away). Four other children, still inside, were burned to death. I had no reason to disbelieve this man when he told me his story. He was about 45 years of age; he said: 'I hope I live long enough to kill four Malays.'

DOCUMENT 22

HUNGARIAN NATIONALISM   *Catechism of the Secret Society of*
Reformers of Hungary, 1794

Q.   How does the Cabinet of Vienna maintain this slavery of the Hungarians?
A.   It keeps Hungarians away from the ministry and council lest they oppose the enslavement of Hungary. All princes of Austria, except Joseph,

in getting Hungarians to sell their freedom have made use of Hungarian prelates, who by their celibacy have ceased to be citizens of their country and who owe their Church preferments to these Austrian rulers. The magnates of Hungary, created by Austria, are induced to live in Vienna, where they slowly develop habits of fawning on the court, and where German women and Viennese courtesans extinguish all love of country in them.

Q.   How is the Hungarian soldier treated by the court of Vienna today?
A.   Most ungratefully. As in the past, Germans and Italians now obtain Hungarian commands, together with most other military ranks, while the Hungarian officer is put off.
Q.   Why does the nefarious court do this?
A.   Because it is afraid that a homogeneous Hungarian army, made up of Hungarians only, would punish its crimes against the Hungarian people.
Q.   Why did Maria Theresa introduce German normal schools in Hungary?
A.   Because she wished to open the way to absolute despotism for Joseph. She hoped that the Hungarian nation would give up its language and in adopting the corrupted language of Austria would also accept their manners and despotism to the ruin of Hungarian liberty.

ACKNOWLEDGMENTS

Illustrations

Popperfoto pages 3, 4 top, 6 bottom, 10, 12, 19; The Mansell
Collection pages 4 bottom, 6 top, 13, 15; Keystone Press
Agency page 9; The Irish Embassy page 14.

Documents

D1, *Masaryk In England,* R.W. Seton Watson, Cambridge
University Press; D4, The Times; D7, *The Great Powers and
the Near East,* M.S. Anderson, Edward Arnold; D8, *Speeches
and Writings of G.K. Gokhale, Volume II,* Asia Publishing
House; D9, *Selected Documents on a History of India and
Pakistan, Volume IV,* ed. C.H. Philips, Oxford University
Press; D12, *Report of the British Guiana Constitutional
Commission,* HMSO; D13, *The West On Trial,* Cheddi Jagan,
Michael Joseph; D16, *Mein Kampf,* Adolph Hitler trans. by
Ralph Mannheim, Hutchinson; D18, *Freedom and After,*
Tom Mboya, André Deutsch; D19, *Freedom and Socialism,*
Julius K. Nyerere, Oxford University Press; D20, *Divide and
Quit,* Penderel Moon, Chatto and Windus; D21, *Malaysia,*
John Slimming, A.M. Heath.

Greenhaven World History Program

History Makers
Alexander
Constantine
Leonardo Da Vinci
Columbus
Luther, Erasmus and Loyola
Napoleon
Bolivar
Adam Smith, Malthus and Marx
Darwin
Bismarck
Henry Ford
Roosevelt
Stalin
Mao Tse-Tung
Gandhi
Nyerere and Nkrumah

Great Civilizations
The Ancient Near East
Ancient Greece
Pax Romana
The Middle Ages
Spices and Civilization
Chingis Khan and the Mongol Empire
Akbar and the Mughal Empire
Traditional China
Ancient America
Traditional Africa
Asoka and Indian Civilization
Muhammad and the Arab Empire
Ibn Sina and the Muslim World
Suleyman and the Ottoman Empire

Great Revolutions
The Neolithic Revolution
The Agricultural Revolution
The Scientific Revolution
The Industrial Revolution
The Communications Revolution
The American Revolution
The French Revolution
The Mexican Revolution
The Russian Revolution
The Chinese Revolution

Enduring Issues
Cities
Population
Health and Wealth
A World Economy
Law
Religion
Language
Education
The Family

Political and Social Movements
The Slave Trade
The Enlightenment
Imperialism
Nationalism
The British Raj and Indian Nationalism
The Growth of the State
The Suez Canal
The American Frontier
Japan's Modernization
Hitler's Reich
The Two World Wars
The Atom Bomb
The Cold War
The Wealth of Japan
Hollywood

Greenhaven World History Program

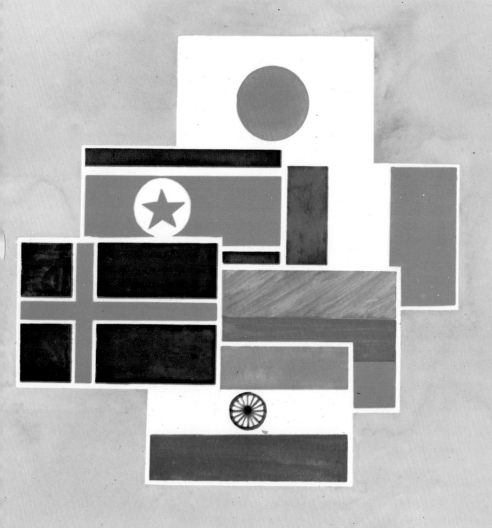